How to Launch a Freelance Copywriting Business

JULES HORNE

Workbook

Want to get your writing business up and running quickly? This step-by-step practical Workbook will help you to cut to the chase.

This Workbook is a companion publication to the Handbook, *How to Launch a Freelance Copywriting Business.*

Join the newsletter at
www.method-writing.com

method writing

Texthouse, The Corn Exchange, 31 Woodmarket, Kelso, TD5 7AT
www.texthouse.co.uk

How to Launch a Freelance Copywriting Business:
Workbook/ Jules Horne. — 2nd ed.

Cover design and typesetting: Victor Marcos
www.99designs.com/profiles/victormarcos/services

ISBN 978-0-9934354-5-4

Contents

Let's Go!

So, you're ready to start your copywriting business, and you've read around on the subject.

But now, you need a roadmap, so you can get going quickly.

That's where this Workbook comes in. This is a practical action plan to accompany my Handbook, *How to Launch a Freelance Copywriting Business*. The *Handbook* has the background knowledge you need for business success. This *Workbook* provides the actions needed to set your business up in easy stages.

Starting a business from scratch can be intense. So this breaks it down. With this Workbook, you'll wear three freelance hats:

- Writing Ninja
- Marketing Ninja
- Operations Ninja

You'll do a little of each role in turn, to keep things manageable. You'll work through practicalities such as:

- building an online presence
- identifying markets to target
- essential and non-essential kit
- establishing a workflow and processes

This Workbook is a companion to my Handbook, *How to Launch a Freelance Copywriting Business*, which includes essential background information. What's in here?

- A step-by-step breakdown of start-up
- A roadmap to follow
- Practical actionable advice

If you follow the steps, you'll be up and running with the basics in a month - maybe less!

The key to business is to dive in, do and learn.

Some people prefer doing lots of learning first, and moving forward when they feel ready. But that way, you could end up six months down the line without making a single sale. This Workbook will get you there much faster.

It's best to keep your process short, sweet, and practical, and learn on the job.

About Me

I'm a commercial and creative writer based in Scotland. Like many writers, I have a freelance portfolio career. I run my own copywriting business, Texthouse, I've written Edinburgh Fringe First-winning plays, BBC radio drama, fiction, and spoken word. I teach part-time on the Open University Creative Writing MA, and co-wrote the Script strand. I'm an ex BBC journalist with a subbing and radio background.

On my path to an independent writing life, I've learned a thing or two that I'd like to pass on. So this book is for younger me, and anyone who wants to put their creative writing skills to work in a business context.

Now to get started!

Operations Ninja 1

Meet your inner Operations Ninja. Your Ops Ninja handles all things admin - a crucial part of your writing business. With solid, clear foundations, you can zoom through your admin and spend far more time on productive writing - the part you really enjoy. Use your Ops Ninja to help you achieve an amazing sense of serenity and write more than you ever thought possible. You'll encounter other ninjas as you go along.

As a business start-up, you have a choice. Either do loads of research, approach your local enterprise organisation, set up a beautiful office and promotional campaign, or...

Cut to the chase.

In most sectors, businesses spend a long time in start-up, laying the foundations, fitting out their premises, putting in systems. They invest a good deal in *getting things right* before they see their first customer.

If you're a shop, a manufacturer, a franchise, you need to do this. You'll probably take out a bank loan, and won't expect to turn a profit for a year or so. Setting things up well will pay dividends down the line.

But as a copywriter, you don't need a lot of infrastructure. This is a low investment, low overhead business. Sure, go the traditional route if you're planning a growth business with employees. But if it's just you, you can go the lean and focused route. Get going quickly, adapt as you go along and learn from your experience.

The approach in this Workbook is based on the business concept of the Minimum Viable Product – the minimum steps you need to get a result, followed by learning and adjustment, also known as *iteration*. So you need to get ready to be decisive, dive in and take action. This workbook will help, by giving you focus.

A legal note

Depending on where you live, you'll have different legal requirements. I'm in the UK, where it's straightforward to set up as a self-employed sole trader. You and the freelance business are the same legal entity. You don't need to be a limited company or VAT registered. If you're in a different country, check out your own set-up.

Enterprise bodies are increasingly aware of the creative freelance workforce. For them, you're like a consultant or independent contractor: a solo service provider, typically working from home.

If contacting your local enterprise support, look for advice aimed at consultants and freelances, rather than bigger companies. If not, you may get traditional industries advice at the wrong scale.

For the purposes of this workbook, I'll assume you're a solo entrepreneur like me.

Disclaimer: As with any businesses, there are no instant guarantees. You need to put the work in and do your own research.

❐ Yes, I understand!

Signed:

Choose a name

Exciting! Your name can be your own, or a trading name. You can still use a trading name as a sole trader. On my tax forms, I'm *Jules Horne trading as (T/A) Texthouse.*

Choosing a good trading or brand name can sometimes take a while. You need something that's easy to say and spell, and simple.

But plenty of business writers trade as themselves, and if you really want to, you can always add a trading name or brand later. So don't overthink it.

If in doubt, use your own name and choose one of the following:

- ❒ *Your Name,* Business & Content Writer
- ❒ *Your Name,* Copywriter
- ❒ *Your Name,* Writing & Editorial Services

Your choice here will depend on the types of businesses nearby. Web-savvy, young and techie businesses typically use "content", while more traditional businesses prefer "business writer". "Copywriter" is sometimes misunderstood outside the creative industries.

If in doubt, choose the first one.

What are you going to put on your business card?

Business or trading name:

Decide your legal status

This is most likely to be (UK) sole trader or (US) sole proprietorship. Check out what's typical in your country.

Legal status:

Your national tax website

This will have information about your obligations. A lot of this may be for far larger businesses - those with separate premises, or which emply people. So don't get overwhelmed. Look out for the information for freelances, sole traders and the self-employed.

National tax website:

Register your business

Find out who you need to notify in your country. This may just be letting them know your self-employment trading name, when you fill in your tax return.

I need to notifiy:

❒ Done

Your business starting date

Decide your business starting date. In the UK, the tax year traditionally starts on 6th April. I chose this starting date for simple alignment with the government tax year. Other people choose the the first of a month, to make monthly reporting easier.

Business starting date:

Make a note of this, as you'll often need it when filling in forms.

Your Unique Tax Reference

You'll need this whenever you fill in forms:

Unique Tax Reference:

Your business bank account

You do need a separate bank account for your business. You could use a separate current account, or opt for a fully fledged business account. Don't be tempted to use the same account as for your personal transactions. Again, you'll need this a lot, so make a note of the details.

Business bank account number: Sort code: Postal address: Bank helpline number:

National Insurance/Social Security Number

As a sole trader, you'll usually need your National Insurance Number (or Social Security Number in the US) when filling in forms. So make a note here:

National Insurance/Social Security Number:

Insurance

Check out what's typical in your country for freelance consultants. I have a professional indemnity and third party insurance package.

Insurance provider and policy:

Marketing Ninja 1

Meet your Marketing Ninja. Your Marketing Ninja gets your message out and connects you with customers. This covers simple steps such as business cards, all the way to websites and promo campaigns. As a sole trader, you don't need to do all of this, but it's good to be aware that some of your tasks come under the "marketing" function.

Now you've got your foundations out of the way, it's time for some fun stuff.

Order business cards

Moo.com is simple, has clear, contemporary designs, and you can order small numbers. Go for a minimalist design, as it'll work for both target businesses and creative colleagues with strong design values. Don't be tempted by clip art. Get the minimum amount.

Don't be tempted by upsells such as complement slips or letterhead paper. You'll rarely need them, as most of your correspondence will be online.

Note: You may want the design to reflect your website colours and fonts. If so, check out Techie Ninja/Branding before you do this.

Keep business cards ready at all times and don't be precious in giving them out. They help to keep you in mind.

❒ Done

Notes:

Choose a website name

This should be aligned with your business name. Choose .com if you can, as it performs better in search. I have my country URL ending, www.texthouse.co.uk, but if I were starting again, I'd go for .com.

This probably won't apply if you're in a country with a different language or your customers are local to your area. If your customers are likely to search using your country URL, choose that.

Many names are already taken, but you can add generic words such as writing services, [yourname]writer, or [yourname] copywriting. Domain names that include relevant search terms may help you to get found more easily, so "writer" or "writing services" can be useful. See the *Handbook*.

Choose something that can be spoken and understood easily on the phone. Trendy spellings that need to be specially explained ("friends with a 'z'") can get on your nerves after a while.

Again, when in doubt, don't overthink it. These things aren't set in stone. You can always choose a new domain name later on and point it to your exisiting site. Your business may evolve as you discover your niche.

I use www.bluehost.com for domain registration. You might have a different or local preference. I find it easiest to have domain registration and website hosting with the same company.

My website name:

Notes:

Technology Ninja 1

Meet your inner Technology Ninja. Your Technology Ninja may be a whiz able to build a simple website. Or, you may have an underpowered Technology Ninja. If that's the case, enlist a professional for jobs like website building. Always check in and be truthful about your skills before trying to DIY. It may cost more to hire a professional, but you'll save a lot of time and effort.

First off: are you a Technology Ninja?

- ❒ Yes (you can build and edit a blog with ease)

Read on. You can build a very simple website. Move on to *Your WordPress Site* below.

- ❒ No (you've never made a hyperlink)

Hire a professional. It'll save money, time and tears in the long term.

For a low-cost solution, try Fivrr. If you have more budget and don't have a local recommendation, try Reedsy, which has curated providers used to working with writers.

Choose a web designer who uses WordPress. Avoid anyone who tries to offer you something else, especially an interface they have designed themselves. If you ever want to move to a different web designer, this makes migration tricky.

Your WordPress site

Yes! Your Techie Ninja is up to the job. Let's get on it.

The good new is, you don't need a big, fancy website as a copywriter. I have a simple one. The main reason to have a website is that businesses will check you out. It's a calling card whose job is to signal your professionalism. If you only have a Facebook presence and no postal address, a serious company may not want to do business with you.

WordPress is the world's biggest website builder. It's used by tiny companies as well as multinationals. There are two versions: WordPress.org (the professional version), and WordPress.com (the free version). Choose WordPress.org.

Some people choose simple site builders such as Wix.com. However, they don't perform as well on search, and it can be hard to migrate your site later on. Unless you're one of those Linux super-ninjas, WordPress is your friend.

Gather your website assets

❒ 100-word biography

Don't overthink. You can improve it later. Remember, we're going for "do, then tweak", rather than "perfection or nothing".

The elements you need are:

Your name and writing experience.

This needs to be as professional as possible. It should also be as relevant as possible to the clients you're trying to attract.

If you have no business writing experience, make the best of writing and editing you've done in previous jobs. Company newsletters, brochures are good. Volunteering for an organisation or group where you've run the newsletter may also be good, as long as it evokes a degree of professionalism.

If you've done journalism, great. Names those media outlets. Clients might also be attracted to your PR potential.

If you're a blogger and it's information-driven and not about your inner life or cat, use that. A tourism site might be good, as long as it looks smart. Journalism-style features are good, too.

Don't use creative writing, poetry, writing for children. These put you in a quite different market. If you have a creative writing degree and have published in magazines, mention it.

As soon as possible, replace weak elements with stronger ones that strengthen your commercial writing profile.

About me:

❒ Photo

Black and white often looks stylish. Again, don't overthink it. Go with what you have, as long as it's friendly and professional. You can always upgrade it later.

❒ 100-word services copy

Don't overpromise. Websites, SEO content, blogs, case studies, editing and print promotions are enough to be going on with.

This covers a lot of ground, and opens up conversations, which is want you want. You'll need to be flexible, but you do need to get the conversation started.

Too many elements will confuse the picture, so it's best to focus on a handful of key ones.

Services:

❒ Contact info

Having a postal address is reassuring for companies, even if you're a small provider. However, businesses will check you out. If a Google search or Google Maps shows pictures of a neglected industrial estate or unreassuring neighbours, don't provide this, or consider a post office box. A quiet residential area is fine, as it's not unusual for copywriters and creatives to work from home. Some countries require a postal address on business websites, though not the UK.

Mobile phones are OK for creatives, too, but see the *Handbook* on phone choices, as there are several considerations.

Your email address should have your domain name. A domain is attached to an ID and address and gives clients a degree of reassurance. Don't use a generic one, such as @gmail.com or @yahoo.com, or you might across as a bot. On no account use a personal, cat or football team-themed one that suggests you're doing this as a sideline.

Address:
Phone number:
Email:

❐ Call to action

A CTA is needed for all the jobs you'll do as a business writer. It's all about asking someone to do something. So decide your CTA for your own site.

What action do you want clients to take? Phone? Email? Get in touch? Fill in a form? Check out your testimonials?

This may change over time. But for this purpose, decide the CTA early on. I find it useful to decide the action verb. It makes writing jobs much easier.

At this stage, it may be as simple as abig button with your phone number or email on it: *Call XXXXX-XXXXX*. Or *Email [your email].* If you like, decide on a separate contact page.

Note: this gathering process is useful for websites you may be called on to write. Corral everything before starting the build. It forces you (and clients) to be clear and decisive, and breaks jobs into manageable chunks.

❐ Contact form

Many websites include a contact form instead of just an email address. There are two main reasons: to cut down spam, and to gather some information from your client. Even a tiny spark of information (I need a article, the company name and website) will help you to get some context and build a picture of the client.

If you're using a form, consider what would be useful. Include no more than 3-4 elements, or an open invitation to describe what they're looking for.

Any detail you can get in a first contact, beyond a name and contact information, is a huge bonus.

Contact form fields/copy:

Branding

Minimalism is always a good choice, as it works for both clients and design colleagues. It also looks more classy and high-end than loud colours and fancy fonts. Simplicity can seem bland to some people, but it's more open to interpretation, and therefore to a wider range of clients and opportunities. A big statement look is limiting your choices, and is more appropriate for a big city agency that can afford to niche right down.

Do also consider whether you have a niche or specialist market. This is about your client market, and not about you. An SEO or technical client won't be attracted to a craft or handmade look. Craftspeople are unlikely to have much money for copywriters, and will often want to write their own creative copy anyway. See the *Handbook* for where you're more likely to find clients with a copywriting budget.

For simplicity, choose one signature colour and neutrals. If you can, pick a web-safe colour, as it'll look more consistent on different screens. Stick to these colours throughout. Note the Hex code of your signature colour, as you'll need it a lot.

❒ Choose branding colours

Hex codes:

Your font is part of your branding, too. It subliminally evokes your business values, and consistency makes you look well put together. Pick something simple - perhaps a body text font and a header font for contrast.

Unusual and custom fonts need different coding on websites, so they can be slower in search results. If you're building the site yourself, choose simple web safe fonts. Make sure your chosen fonts are also available in your Word programme.

Sans-serif web safe fonts: Arial, Verdana, Trebuchet MS, Tahoma, Arial Black.

Serif web safe fonts: Times New Roman, Georgia, Palatino, Lucida Bright, Garamond.

❒ Choose fonts

Header font: Body text font:

The build

This will take some time, but will be much quicker if you gather the assets before hand. Here are the main steps.

Email can either be hosted by your domain (usually you include this in your package), or you can forward your domain email to a forwarding address such as @gmail.com.

I prefer the professional approach of purchasing domain, email and hosting in one package.

- ❒ Buy your domain name and hosting package, with email if you want. I use www.bluehost.com.
- ❒ Create your landing page
- ❒ Add your copy
- ❒ Add your image
- ❒ Add your contact details
- ❒ Decide whether you want a blog module to complement your main pages, and add this if so.
- ❒ Publish
- ❒ Check
- ❒ Contact your provider (e.g. Bluehost to link your site to your domain.
- ❒ Get them to help with email setup if needed.
- ❒ Wait a couple of days for it to perpetuate across the web.

- ❒ Check using your proper domain name.
- ❒ Test sending and receiving emails using that address.
- ❒ Set up this email in your Microsoft Outlook, if you're using Office.

LinkedIn

LinkedIn is the primary social media platform for businesses. Facebook is mainly for personal socialising and Twitter is for chatting. These to can become a tremendous distraction and take a huge amount of effort to do well. You don't need to go there, unless you really want to.

Facebook can work well for lifestyle, consumer and community businesses. But as a copywriter, you're a B2B business. Your business is other businesses. They're unlikely to be hanging out on social media and looking for copywriters there.

I rarely use social media. It stops me getting on with productive work, and I've never met clients through it. But if I were starting out today, I'd at least join LinkedIn, wearing my marketing hat.

- ❒ Join LinkedIn

Your LinkedIn handle:

Outlook email signature

Your Outlook email signature needs your contact information and branding. Later, you'll set up more for different situations

- ❐ Set up your Outlook email and signature

Notes:

Operations Ninja 2

Procurement is one of the most fun parts of the job. You get to buy kit and software! However, procurement needs seriously kept in check. Here are some of the key items you need. You probably have most of them already. The aim here is to get you started quickly, so don't buy more until you're up and running. Read the *Handbook* for more on Kit & Caboodle.

This may just be a checklist, if you have these items already. If so, great! Tick them off and move on. See the *Handbook* for tech specs and options, especially about computers and software, and especially if you're a Mac user.

- ❒ Computer
- ❒ Broadband internet
- ❒ Microphone headset
- ❒ Microsoft 365
- ❒ Webcam (if you don't have a built-in one)

Microsoft 365 has all the Office applications you'll need - Word, Outlook, Excel, possibly Powerpoint and Teams.

This is a subscription cloud-based service with additional downloads of the latest version of the software to your local computer.

This means you're always up to date and can access it anywhere.. I highly recommend this if you don't already have Microsoft 365.

❒ Get Microsoft 365

Your writing space

Again, you probably have this in place. See the *Handbook* for more on this.

Don't forget this is your job, so you need office-style desk and chair heights.

❒ Office-height table
❒ Office-style heigh-adjustable chair
❒ A desk light

Your phone

You'll need to keep personal and professional calls separate. Web-based Zoom and Skype calls are another option. See the *Handbook* for more on this.

❒ Phone

Notes:

Writing Ninja 1

Now you have a website, you can start talking about what you do. The next stage is to establish social proof of your skills. You can achieve this through testimonials, writing samples or case studies of how you've helped a company by writing for them. See the *Handbook* for more on breaking the chicken-and-egg cycle of needing work samples in order to get work.

Do you have commercial writing samples?

❒ Yes
❒ No

If no, head to *Portfolio Samples*.
If yes, choose one of the following to post on your website:

❒ Sample paragraphs on your website
❒ Case study explaining what you did for the client.

Sample 1:

Sample 2:

Sample 3:

A case study is written up and has a typical structure. It's more involved, but shows a specific example of your services and ideally will include a client testimonial.

As a writer, you'll find it easy to do this.

Case study template

What is the theme?
What problem did you solve? Launch, new market, repositioning...

What were things like before your help?
The "before" part of the picture.

What were things like after your help?
The "after" part of the picture.

Client comments to corroborate what you say:

Do you have client testimonials?

❒ Yes

Put them on your website.

❒ No, but I can ask for some

Contact likely companies and start gathering testimonials. They're gold! Set up a Word document just for these.

❒ No.

Set up a Word document anyway.

Starter projects

☞ These ***Starter Projects*** are for writers who have never done paid copywriting before. They will ease you in gently, and equip you with a bunch of portfolio pieces to show clients or put on your website.

This section has some assignments designed to kickstart your portfolio. Do these, and you'll end up with your own leaflet and a couple of good-looking samples to show. You can then start reaching out to paid clients, and building a work pipeline. See more about these assignments in the *Handbook*.

Most writers have samples they can adapt, so these are included in an appendix at the back of this book.

❒ No need for Starter Projects
❒ Assignment 1 - Flyer
❒ Assignment 2 - Client Flyer
❒ Assignment 3a - Speculative Sample
❒ Assignment 3b - Real Job, Real Client
❒ Assignment 4 - Case Study
❒ Assignment 5 - Case Study

Put them on your website.

Marketing Ninja 2

Your next Marketing Ninja job is to start looking for work and promoting yourself. The aim long-term is to build a work pipeline so work comes your way, and you don't have to do constant promotion. So in this section, you'll approach some potential referrers and design collaborators, and start to build a leads list.

Referrals

See the Handbook section on *Referrals* and brainstorm people who may be able to help you. These may be former clients or people you've worked with.

Don't worry if you can't think of anyone right now. Over time, you'll ask clients for referrals and build your reach that way.

Referral brainstorm:

1.

2.

3.

4.

5.

Email them to say you're starting a copywriting business, remind them of the work you've done for them (as long as it wasn't over a year ago), and ask if they'd be happy to help you out.

- ❐ Referrer 1
- ❐ Referrer 2
- ❐ Referrer 3
- ❐ Referrer 4
- ❐ Referrer 5

Design collaborators

A professional design collaborator can be a great help for building a steady work pipeline. These can be web or graphic designers, who are often the first port of call for clients looking for a new website or print materials. They may be able to send work your way.

So start by identifying professional colleagues whose work you like and who also provide B2B services. This is a long-term process of relationship-building, but it can pay dividends in the long term. See more about what kind of designers (web and graphic) to look out for in the *Handbook*.

Design collaborators:

1.

2.

3.

4.

5.

Now email each one, follow them on LinkedIn, and explain that you're saying hello as a copywriting startup looking for design colleagues to collaborate with, and something positive about their work.

Don't be pushy about this. Your first step is to make them aware of you, not to sell direct. You may be lucky! But at this stage, you're relationship-building. If they're looking for someone for future, they'll check out your website.

- ❒ Designer 1
- ❒ Designer 2
- ❒ Designer 3
- ❒ Designer 4
- ❒ Designer 5

Other potential referrers

Some other B2B types of businesses may be a good complement for your services, especially those that work with a lot of other businesses.

For example, accountants have a lot of business clients, as do business hubs and others. In some cases, there will be initial trust and confidentiality issues that may disallow them from referring you directly. But they may also be interested to hear about a business writing service in their area, for future reference. So don't hesitate to reach out and make them aware of you. Again, don't try to sell directly. It's early days in your relationship.

Referrer brainstorm:

1.

2.

3.

4.

5.

Notes:

Operations Ninja 3

In this section, you'll look at putting systems in place to streamline your admin workflow. This includes general office systems, and a workflow process for handline incoming jobs.

This section is about keeping your work and office routines corraled, so that you keep track of work in progress, and know where to find key items.

You will naturally evolve your own system and tools. However, I'm offering mine here, as I've honed them over the years, and after a lot of trial and error, they now work well for me.

One of the challenges of the writing job is the need to go deep into the focus mindspace for productive work, yet frequently surface to to manage phone calls, admin and other small interruptions.

Many writers find this focus-pulling hard. Systems can make this easier to deal with.

Operations Manual

An ops manual is a folder where you gather systems and routines you use repeatedly. I use a ring binder for this, as it's easy to retrieve from the shelf and I can scribble changes in it. You can add to it over time.

- ❒ Set up Operations Manual (ring binder or Word document).
- ❒ Insert category dividers. Mine include jobs, passwords, video, audio, work processes and finance.

When I want to add something, I take a note, then update the Ops Manual about once a month.

Weekly meeting sheet

At the start of each week, decide priorities, check what invoices are due and need to be chased, what meetings and deadlines are ahead week, and what jobs need to be progressed.

Since I now work with my partner, we use a meeting sheet as the basis for our weekly meeting.

It takes half an hour to check the finances, see what's outstanding, remind ourselves of upcoming commitments and bottlenecks, and plan the week's focus.

I use the concept of big rocks, pebbles and gravel to block in major goals and small jobs, and note "waiting for" jobs and new tasks as they come in .

Each week, we review the successes of the last week, what jobs have been carried over, and any invoices outstanding.

This provides a watertight overview of work in progress, so it's harder to lose track of things while you're immersed in writing.

Note small jobs and interruptions on the sheet so that they can be addressed in a batch, so you don't lose your writing or editing flow.

- ❒ Set up a weekly meeting sheet.
- ❒ Print out copies and keep in your Ops Manual.

Kanban board

A kanban board is a big whiteboard with a visual representation of jobs and the flow of time. Each job or task has a job ticket, and these are grouped and moved around as work progresses. This helps to keep work in view and on track.

You may prefer a different or digital system. However, I find this a very good way to work out your process. It's flexible - just paper slips on a whiteboard marked into areas. Over time, you can adjust and regroup your priorities in a way that makes sense to you. So I suggest you try kanban for a few weeks, at least.

My kanban board has a large "waiting for" area for jobs that need answers from clients, quotes that need approval, or items due to be delivered. This helps me to focus on work that I can progress.

The board is checked at the beginning and end of each day, and items moved or removed as required. When resurfacing after a period of writing,

If you feel a kanban board would be useful, set one up. Your categories can be provisional to start with, and changed as your system evolves. Using dry markers means nothing is set in stone.

- ❒ Get a large whiteboard, dry markers and cleaning cloth.
- ❒ Fix the whiteboard to the wall.
- ❒ Make job slips, or use sticky notes for jobs and tasks.
- ❒ Decide on categories or boxes and mark up the board. Mine include *quotes, jobs in progress, waiting for, ready to invoice,* and *invoices outstanding.*

Job folders

Job folders or cardboard wallets are needed for the paperwork on each job. This can include research, briefing notes, and drafts in progress. Staple on a copy of the job ticket and client contact information, including phone and website logons, if you need them.

Decide an area for keeping "live" folders - jobs still to be completed and invoiced - and "completed" - paid jobs that have completed their workflow.

I use a system of clipboards for each job. Each job gets a clipboard to hold all notes and papers. If there's a lot of attached research paperwork, I use a wallet folder.

- ❐ Get wallet folders.
- ❐ Get clipboards, if you want them.

Job number system

A job number system is a great help for keeping your work on track. My productivity and focus has improved greatly since using one.

Allocate a job number once the work has been agreed, and use it through the workflow in:

- job slip
- job document titles
- email headers
- online file folder
- physical job folder or clipboard
- invoice.

I use a formula like this:

INS-101 SEO

INS - unique abbreviation of the company name
101 - three-digit number
PRESS RELEASE - memorable identifier.

Other examples:

BLI-123 AD
NAT-119 BLOGS APRIL

The code BLI-123 follows the job throughout your workflow, making it easy to find attached files in Dropbox, your accounts, invoices and client emails.

- ❐ Decide on a job naming convention.
- ❐ Create an Excel spreadshee for jobs.

Job tickets

Jobs tickets on a kanban board are one good way to keep track of workflow. My job tickets include the job number code and space for adding notes, such as invoice date. Job ticket software is an overspec if you only have a few jobs on the go at the same time. Also, I prefer reminders to be kept in view. For digital alternatives, see the *Handbook*.

- ❐ Design a simple job ticket with space for job code and notes.
- ❐ Print some copies and keep them by your kanban board.

Phone book

Set up your mobile and landline with key phone numbers you're likely to use at work. Add a Favourite star to any regulars.

This has the advantage you'll be able to see who is making incoming calls. Make a habit of doing this with new clients, especially if they're likely to become regulars.

- ❐ Update your landline phone book.
- ❐ Update your mobile phone book and add Favourites.
- ❐ Post your own and any emergency numbers on the wall where you can see them.

Wall info sheet

Some numbers and information are best kept close to hand, either because you use them regularly, or because you'll need them in an emergency.

I keep useful numbers and information pinned on the wall and inside my diary. Phone number and postcode are a must. Also include work, family and emergency medical numbers, National Insurance and broadband logon numbers. Don't do this if your office is public facing.

- ❐ Put a list of VIP numbers and info on the wall.
- ❐ Put this list in your planner.

Notes:

So you've now set up the main office systems you need. Now to put back on your Marketing Ninja hat.

Marketing Ninja 3

For your next step as a Marketing Ninja, it's time to tackle your elevator pitch and think about how to present yourself when speaking to others. This is so that you come across well and practise explaining what you do, succinctly and clearly.

Elevator Pitch

"What do you do?" is a common question, yet it can catch you unawares. Write out and practise your elevator pitch. This will help you hone your business vision at the same time. Be prepared to evolve your elevator pitch along with your business, and adapt it to different situations.

Elevator pitch:

One Way to Formulate an Elevator Pitch

Identify the customer and their pain point. ("You know when businesses commission a new website and struggle with what to put in it?")

Explain what you do. ("I take their raw information and write stylish SEO web content...")

Explain the value of what you do. ("...so that they get found easily on the web, and customers find information that helps them decide whether to buy.")

This is an SEO example. Depending on your copywriting niche and skills, you'll come up with something different.

Presentation

Maybe you don't need to think about presentation, and are already stylish and well groomed, with a lovely home you're proud to show on camera.

However, the aim of this Workbook is to help reduce the amount of thinking you do upfront, so that you can spend more time on productive writing. Particularly in this Zoom era, with greater blurring between personal and business lives, it's helpful to give some thought to your dress code and suroundings.

If you're appearing on webcam, you may want to identify or purchase a few go-to items you can rely on to make you look the part at short notice. This may include keeping a hairbrush, scarf and makeup handy.

Workwear:

Items to keep handy:

Need to buy:

❒ Yes, I'm ready.

Presentation

It's also helpful to think through your Zoom surroundings and decor. Do you have a backdrop, setup and lighting that work for you, and where you can take a call at short notice? Or are you relying on a pile of wobbly books to hold your laptop? And unflattering backlighting? Do you have a microphone headset to improve your sound quality?

Useful items I use include a riser stand for my laptop, a Bluetooth keyboard so I can type while it's on the stand, and an extra light. Sometimes people use a ring light. I also use a microphone headset (USB) or an earbud microphone (minijack). Check how you look and sound on screen, and identify anything you still need.

Video source: **Audio source:**   **Lighting:**   **Set dressing props:**   **Need to buy:**

- ❒ Zoom corner chosen.
- ❒ Lighting tested.
- ❒ Video tested.
- ❒ Audio tested.
- ❒ Set dressed and tested.
- ❒ Yes, I'm ready.

It can be useful to gather settings and other notes that can get forgotten in the heat of the moment.

The Checklist Manifesto by Atul Gawande is a great book on the power of checklists for streamlining your process. Especially if you're plugging around different phones, USB devices and earphones, or other family members use your computer, your settings can come unstuck. I always do a quick check on audio and video sources before starting a Zoom or Teams call. Make a note here of anything you need to remember about your process.

Notes:

Operations Ninja 4

In this section, you'll put computer workflow systems in place.

☞ NB Computer hardware and software are covered in the Handbook in ***Kit & Caboodle***.

Browser setup

Save time by setting up bookmarks for pages you use all the time. I use Google Chrome. Use the Bookmark Manager to create folders to reflect your workflow needs. Mine include Admin/Finance, My Sites, Client Sites and How-To/Learning.

- ❒ Set up brower tabs and folders.

Security setup

Cybersecurity is a big consideration these days. It's imperative to have security and anti-virus software. I use McAfee, but there are others.

- ❒ Get and install computer security package.
- ❒ Install it on your other devices (phone, tablet).

It's also a good idea to use a dedicated password manager which allows you to use multiple complex passwords that would be impossible to memorise, but are much safer. I use 1Password, and again, there are others. Google's own password manager is helpful but not as secure as a dedicated product.

- ❒ Get and install a password manager.
- ❒ Commit to never using the same password twice.

Online storage

If you have Office 365, you already have OneDrive and Sharepoint. These are both Microsoft online cloud storage areas similar to Dropbox. See the *Handbook* for more about this.

I use online storage for most everyday work and backup, and solid state external hard drives for historical files, and occasionally very large files such as video.

As a start-up, you don't really need more than this.

However, it's a good idea to get used to draft versions, so you don't inadvertently overwrite your only copy of an important file. Office saves files automatically, so this is a real danger.

- ❒ Decide on your cloud storage (probably OneDrive).
- ❒ Get a solid state external drive if you need one.

Filing system

A hierarchical filing system is great for finding things easily, and it makes your business easier to scale. Job numbers are also great for searching quickly for files.

You'll have your own preferences, but here's the setup I use, in conjunction with paper filing and a kanban board.
ese sub-folders:

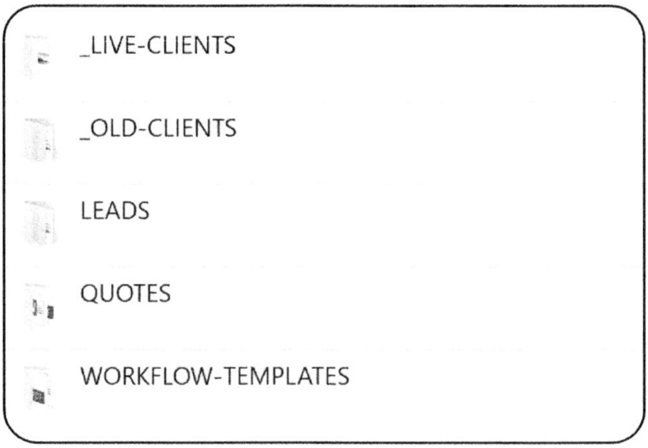

- LIVE - for client work in progress
- OLD - for clients not currently in the pipeline.
- LEADS - for leads and inquiries
- QUOTES - for current and previous quotes
- TEMPLATES - workflow documents

This is backed by a parallel file hierarchy in Outlook:

- LIVE CLIENTS
- OLD CLIENTS
- LEADS
- QUOTES

- ❐ Set up online folder hierarchy.
- ❐ Set up Outlook folder hierarchy.

Other kit

See **Kit & Caboodle** in the *Handbook* for more on this.
These are items I find indispensible. A spare laptop power cable means I can keep one in the office and one at home, and don't need to carry it around and potentially damage it. And USB and SD cards are great for transfering files. Decide whether they're useful for your situation and budget.

- ❐ Get spare cable.
- ❐ Get USB or SD card.

Kaizen list

The Japanese art of *kaizen* means tiny incremental improvements to smooth your businesses and reduce friction. Over time, these small steps will make your workflow more efficient. Note your ideas below.

- ❐ On your landline phone, mark the "handsfree" button.
- ❐ Mark the "mute" button.
- ❐ Mark the "transfer call" button.

Kaizen list:

Writing Ninja 2

Follow this section when doing your first business assignment or Starter Project (see Appendix). This will help you to set up your writing workflow, templates and other time-saving processes.

Writing

The writing process is different for everyone, so you'll want to find what works best for you. I find it useful to break it down into stages, so that you're not thinking of everything at once.

For your first assignment, set up sub-folders within your LIVE_CLIENT folder:

- GATHER - for briefing notes, research materials
- DRAFTS - for drafts in progress
- IMAGES - for photos, logos
- TECH - for passwords, technical specs

Put contracts and financial information in your general ADMIN folder, not separate client folders. This is a job for your Operations Ninja, not your Writing Ninja!

❒ Set up a blank folder group for a client.

❒ Duplicate this and name it with your first job code.

Template 1 - Letterhead

It's best to work with templates to save time, and to make your work look professional. Your letterhead needs:

- business name and address
- logo, if you have one
- email
- phone number

Microsoft has business letterheads you can use. This can be customized with:

- your font
- brand colours
- logo, if you have one

❒ Set up Template 1 - Letterhead
❒ Add an area for job code

Template 2 - SEO Blog

A blog template is another useful timesaver, and will give your blog drafts a professional finish. You can add other useful templates over time. Copy Template 1, and add in areas for:

- keyword phrase
- metadescription
- header 1
- header 2
- call to action
- hyperlinks

❒ Set up Template 2 - SEO Blog

See the *Handbook* for the revision and client sign-off process.

Operations Ninja 5

This takes you into financial and legal territory. This rarely comes naturally to writers and other creatives, but clear foundations can really help reduce stress and is a basic business foundation. Without these elements, you'll find it hard to grow. So let's go for it.

Book-keeping

The secret to book-keeping sanity is "little and often." To keep record-keeping under control, either update transactions right away, or book a dedicated hour in your diary each week. Stick to your commitment, and stay up to date.

You can use a simple Excel spreadsheet, a ring binder with poly pockets for receipts, or online software complete with phone capture for receipts. I started with the first kind, and graduated eventually to Xero software and a bookkeeper. This was worth the investment, as it saved time and headaches. See the *Handbook* for more on this.

- ❐ Choose your record-keeping system
- ❐ Set up a FINANCE folder online

- ❒ Set up a [relevant tax year] sub-folder
- ❒ Under that, add INCOME and EXPENSES folders
- ❒ Add any expenses sub-groups you need
- ❒ Decide a process for capturing petty cash receipts
- ❒ Commit to a weekly book-keeping slot in your diary.

Template 3 - Quote

See the *Handbook* section on **Quotes, Estimates, Ballparks** and **Rates**.

- ❒ Set up Template 3 - Quote
- ❒ Decide your day rate
- ❒ Decide your hourly rate

Notes:

Letter of engagement

This is a short contract which both parties agree to, to allow the job to proceed.

Initially, it's OK to use a simply worded exchange of emails. You can set this up as an email signature in Outlook (a useful tip for boilerplate emails).

Down the line, you'll probably want to migrate to a separate document with online signature, as it's more professional and formal. This will especially apply if you start working with bigger companies. I use Adobe software for this.

- ❐ Decide wording for your Letter of Engagement
- ❐ Set this up as an email signature in Outlook

Billing and reminder emails

Write a short series of polite emails for billing and follow-up. As above, you can create these as email signatures in Outlook.

- ❐ "Here's your invoice" email
- ❐ Gentle follow-up 1
- ❐ Sterner follow-up 2

Terms & conditions

Decide your terms of doing business. This will typically cover payment terms, number of revisions, copyright, and what happens in the event of problems, illness or other tricky circumstances.

Read some examples online. Often, they're in the footer section of websites. In some countries, it's obligatory to put T&Cs on your website. You may require legal advice to get the right official wording.

- ❒ Compile or commission Terms & Conditions
- ❒ Add this to your website (usually the footer section)

Data protection notice

In the UK, all businesses handling data need to register as a data holder with the Information Commissioner's Office (ICO). Check what's required in your country.

- ❒ Register with the ICO or your national equivalent

Accountants

You'll need someone to handle your end-of-year tax return. In the UK, book-keepers can do this. As you grow your business, you'll probably want a dedicated accountant.

It's a good idea to ask creative contacts about this. You don't want to pay over the odds for a swish accountant that normally deals with big companies.

Notes:

Marketing Ninja 4

This about finding clients. At this point, writer paths diverge, as every writer and every situation is different. You need to analyse your own skills, contacts, previous employment, specialisms and appetite for networking, businesses and sectors on the doorstep, and opportunities ahead. All these factors will have a bearing on what work you can find. Others writers find opportunities online. So this section is about brainstorming opportunities, and getting the message out more widely.

Finding clients

Read **A Creative's Guide to Business** in the *Handbook* and note your findings about markets, sectors, scales of business and the SME sweet spot. This is really important groundwork for a copywriting start-up, and you need to identify where this information overlaps with your skills and opportunities.

What have you learned about the SME sweetspot?

What industries are in your local area?

What do you know about SEO writing?

By this point, you have a leaflet, website, email signature and letterhead, and have contacted some potential referrers. You've written or compiled a couple of portolio pieces, too. If a reasonable amount of time has passed (say, a couple of weeks), follow up again.

❒ Follow up with potential referrers

Now is a great time to do a SWOT analysis of strengths, weaknesses, opportunities and threats, to get a handle on what's unique about you and your situation.

You might identify, for example, that you have a university technology park on the doorstep, or that a former employer is looking for freelance support. Maybe former colleagues are starting up a business, or someone needs help with a case study or a website copymakeover. These are all good starting points.

❒ Complete a SWOT analysis

Strengths:	**Weaknesses:**

Opportunities:	Threats:

Sales funnel

Sales people refer to the "sales funnel" - a process of converting strangers into leads, warm prospects, clients and eventually fans and advocates.

When you're a start-up, most people are strangers. Your task is to move them along the funnel, step by step.

It's important not to go into full-on sales mode when someone is a stranger. They aren't warm to you yet. They'll run a mile. You have to earn their trust by proving your worth to them.

Most businesses have some kind of customer relationship management system (CRM) to support this. It may be just an Excel spreadsheet, or it may be a full bells-and-whistles dedicated piece of software.

At this stage, you just need an Excel spreadsheet with names, contact information, and categories of LEAD, PROSPECT and CLIENT, with a column for notes and dates.

❐ Set up an Excel CONTACT spreadsheet.

Build your list

It's easier and more productive to start where you are, and build from people you already know. That way, there's already a degree of trust and connection. So it's time to start brainstorming from your wider circle, including what you've discovered from your SWOT analysis.

Approaching people can feel a stretch, but you need to get used to this, if you want to run a business.

First, make a list of individuals. Other business people are more likely to be familiar with referrals, so that's a good starting point. Don't underestimate your extended family, as people you may meet only occasionally at family gatherings might be in business themselves, and interested in supporting you.

Business people:

Business advisers:

Former colleagues:

Friends:

Family:

To start with, pick 10 of the most promising people, add them to list. Send them an email explaining about your new businesses.

❒ Send prospect emails.

In parallel, make a list of nearby companies. The *Handbook* has tips on the scale and nature of company that might be a good fit. SMEs, NGOs, charities and local government have different ways of working and hiring service contractors. Not all are open to small start-ups, and some have better budgets than others. But if you have a direct connection or experience, e.g. in third sector or an industry specialism, this is highly relevant.

SMEs:

Charities:

NGOs:

Sectors

If you have a technical specialism such as IT or engineering, and can communicate complexity to a general audience, this may be a good niche. Often, there's a gap between the technical side and decision-makers (e.g. procurement) that needs to be bridged effectively.

Mature industries such as farming, finance and accountancy can be slow to change, and are often risk-averse. Others are in a fast-changing culture and call for a different approach. B2C/B2B and urban/rural are other differentiators. Make a list of sectors you can build a link to.

Note that you don't need to know everything about the industry. Like a journalist, you'll learn as you go along. For copywriting, it's usually most productive to work with the client's words and expertise.

Technical industries:
Engineering, IT, environmental.

Traditional industries:
Hospitality, tourism, manufacturing.

Other:

Writing Ninja 3

The writing process is different for everyone. You'll probably do a mix of gathering (research), drafting, and proofing. Some jobs, especially websites, have a typical structure, and lend themselves to templates. So it can be helpful to set up some processes to speed things up and keep the job manageable. Packages can also help to give clients a helpful steer. Work through this section to get an overview of the steps, and develop a process that works for you.

Onboarding process

So far, you've set up a Letter of Engagement, to get the client relationship underway on a solid footing.

The next step is an onboarding process. This doesn't need to be complex - an email outlining what's next is fine. This is reassuring for the client, and will help you both to be more efficient.

Part of your job is to manage incoming information from the client. It's easy for them to send you emails with lots of file attachments or copy you in on email chains to others. This can quickly get out of hand.

Everything you receive takes time to process, which costs you time and money. So you need to take the iniative and explain what you need, so that you don't get overwhelmed by incoming.

Useful steps to agree with the client include email handling:

- use the job reference in emails
- use bullet points where possible
- one designated point of contact
- no long "copy to" chains

- ❒ Decide your email handling needs
- ❒ Write this up for your onboarding email (keep it short)

Notes:

Gathering process

Certain types of documents and resources are helpful for getting a sense of the company quickly. They include

- company promotional material
- company website
- copy from tendering applications (business-facing)
- key competitor websites

It's good to read these before you have a scoping conversation, as they'll give you important background, concepts and terminology. Remember to ask how they refer to customers. They might be *clients, visitors* or *service users*, for example.

- ❐ Decide your gathering process
- ❐ Decide where you'll gather documents

Notes:

Briefing process

For briefing, schedule a phone call to fill in background and scope the job, in terms of either word counts or time.

Many jobs have an iterative process of to-and-fro, with the client filling in information gaps as you go along. So it's good to clarify that this is normal.

You can make the briefing process more effective in a number of ways.

- simple list of questions
- telephone interview sheet
- online questionnaire

Each of these will help you focus, save time, and reassure the client. An online questionnaire will also allow you to gather the key information in writing, and help your client to be more decisive. This will free up your phone call for the detail.

You can always start off with a simple form, and migrate to an online questionnaire later on. Some people also find online scheduling software helpful. Microsoft 365 has a Bookings app included.

- ❐ Decide on your briefing approach
- ❐ Write up your briefing questions
- ❐ Decide on a scheduling process

Notes:

Drafting process

Journalists often write to specific word counts to fill a designated space. This is a helpful approach for copywriters, too, whether working for print or web. See the *Handbook* for information on different types and scopes of job you might encounter.

When scoping the job, establish a rough word count. Short and long blogs are different forms. Case studies can be a page long, or cover several pages, go into technical detail and involve client interviews.

So it's important to frame the job clearly. If you think you're likely to write a specific kind of job often, create a template.

- ❐ Establish job and cost parameters for blogs (long), blogs (short) and case studies (long and short)
- ❐ Create templates for these

Notes:

Revision process

A clear revision process will help you to manage a clear to-and-fro with your client. Big website projects in particular can quickly become unwieldly. It's good to take the lead on managing this.

Establish a single designated point of contact within a company. If they're a bigger company likely to send contributions from different people, ask whether they have Sharepoint for gathering and collating. With smaller companies and only one point of contact, it's fine to use email file attachments and save them out to OneDrive.

Establish revision conventions and a Style Guide to save time and arguments. Choose one with an online version, so that you can send a link to clients. I use the *Oxford University Style Guide*, which has simple and minimalist conventions. In other countries, you'll want to use your local conventions.

With Word documents, use a naming convention for different draft versions, and explain this to the client. Never delete the old versions until the job is completed and paid for. I use the file naming convention:

BRO-103 TOPIC v1 Jan 3 JH

Breaking it down:

[jobcode+keyword] + [version] + [date] + [initials]

Client Jim Smith's version will come back as

BRO-103 TOPIC v2 Jan 5 JS

- ❒ Decide how and where files will be sent and shared
- ❒ Decide on a file draft naming convention
- ❒ Add this to your briefing document

How files will be shared:

Where files will be shared:

Naming convention:

Editing passes

Editing happens at different scales, from big structural edits, to line edits, to fine-grained proofing. Although these processes overlap and interweave a lot, it's often more efficient to break them down.

Editing passes are just a check run focusing on a single issue, such as punctuation, layout or spelling consistency. Separate passes helps to create a degree of detachment, and ensures you don't miss details.

Many proofreaders use a sheet of paper to cover up the text and reveal a line at a time. This is similar - you're creating the conditions for focus, rather than scanning.

With editing passes, you can zoom through each one quickly, check it off, and move on to the next one, which is much quicker than scanning for every issue at once. Useful content checks include:

- name, address, postal/zip code, contact email
- call to action
- prices
- company or charity number
- table of contents

Editing passes might include:

- capitalization
- quotation marks
- paragraph indents
- hyphenation
- extra or missing spaces

❒ Make a list of editing passes

Notes:

Job sign-off

It's important for both sides to agree when the job is finished, so that you can send your bill. Jobs can sometimes get stuck in limbo if the client doesn't have time to make final checks, or needs to run it past someone else in their organisation. This puts you on the back foot, as it leaves you waiting for someone's input you have no control over.

This can be managed with a (for example) 50% upfront + 50% on delivery agreement. If you choose to do this, you can factor it into your onboarding process. This is a good idea with large projects.

Or, if the job is all but signed off, send your final invoice, adding an hour or so to accommodate any final checks. Then your payment won't get stalled.

- ❐ Decide your sign-off process
- ❐ Decide whether to request an upfront amount
- ❐ Build this into your onboarding process

Notes:

Packages

Packages can save time in the long run. Clarifying your terms, costs and process for a job likely to be repeated will help your client, too. Start by developing one or two packages.

- ❒ Decide on a package you want to offer
- ❒ Scope and cost it
- ❒ Write up your offer
- ❒ Post it on your website
- ❒ Repeat with a second package

Notes:

Operations Ninja 6

You're already doing a kaizen process of constant small improvements to your workflow. This section is about similar tweaks to improve your bottom line. It will be most useful once you've done a few jobs and developed your process.

Improve your bottom line

For freelances, the main limitation on earning more income is your time. So, breaking it down as a sole trader, there are really only a few ways to improve your bottom line:

- work longer hours (time)
- work harder (intensity)
- work smarter (efficiency)
- cut costs
- charge more
- get more sales

The first three are about process, and the second three about money. Each of these is a point of leverage where adjustments can be made to your business. So let's look at these in turn:

Work longer hours (time)

You need to first to establish where your time is going. Logging your hours for a week can be revealing. As a business freelance, you need to maximise time spent on productive work - work with a billable output. Look at the proportion of billable and non-billable hours, and in particular, minimise unproductive "busy work" where you may be wasting time.

Typical time-drains include social media, meetings, tackling minor admin and answering emails, before paid work. One issue for me is the need to "go dark" for writing productivity, and the danger of meanwhile dropping the ball on admin. Speedy and reactive tasks such as emails also take up more time than they need to.

Many freelances use time-blocking to manage this. The Pomodoro Technique of 25-minute bursts of work, interspersed with clusters of admin jobs, can help. I use Toggl software. See **Managing Your Workload** in the *Handbook*.

- ❒ Log your work hours for a week
- ❒ Analyse areas for improvement
- ❒ Decide next actions

Notes:

Work harder (intensity)

Are you working hours productive and focused? When you work on your own, it's easy to drift. I use industrial earmuffs and sometimes kitchen timers, when focus is a struggle. Full-on work also needs to be counterbalanced with breaks, or diminishing returns can set in. Stepping away from the keyboard entirely will refresh your brain and often your writing. Read the *Handbook* section and see where you can make changes.

- ❐ Decide your most productive writing time
- ❐ Decide what productivity tools would help
- ❐ Plan your schedule with non-negotiable breaks

Notes:

Work smarter (efficiency)

Freelances typically make more income from doing larger projects, repeat jobs for the same client, or work in a sector where they have experience. Look out for opportunities where you can scale or develop your work pipeline, rather than reinventing the wheel with new clients each time.

- ❒ Brainstorm ideas for upsells or extra services
- ❒ Brainstorm ideas for using your expertise
- ❒ Decide next actions

Notes:

Cut costs

Copywriting is one of the lowest overhead businesses around. But you may be tempted to splash out on office furniture, gadgets, stationery, or start subscriptions that continue for months, without being used enough. Some items may be right for a later stage of your business, when you're starting to scale, but not for start-up.

- ❒ Analyse your expenses and see what can be cut
- ❒ Check subscriptions and whether you're using them enough
- ❒ Cut what you can

Notes:

Charge more

Consider putting up your rates, especially as you gain experience. It can be useful to map time against earnings for each job, and analyse what kinds of work earn you more for your time. Some projects and clients are prone to scope creep, leaving you with little margin for your good efforts. Others are so short that the time taken to onboard the client isn't worth it. In this case, you could offer the client editing or proofing services instead, or field the job to someone else. Read the *Handbook* section on rates.

- ❐ Identify where you can increase margin
- ❐ Identify what jobs to avoid
- ❐ Decide how to deflect jobs you don't want
- ❐ Decide on next actions

Notes:

Get more sales

First, check your capacity. There's no point in bringing in more work if you can't turn it around quickly and efficiently. To grow sales, start by upselling to existing clients. Beyond that, reach out to people on your Contacts list, which you should be updating as you go along.

- ❒ Identify potential upsells
- ❒ Identify promising leads
- ❒ Consider limited offers or incentives
- ❒ Decide on next actions

Notes:

Business growth

Once you've fully realized the potential of your own time, the only way to grow is to leverage the time of others. Employing others is beyond the scope of this Workbook, but it's good to consider as a possible direction.

The E-Myth by Michael Gerber is a great foundational book on business growth. It brilliantly describes the usual pitfalls faced by small businesses who want to grow. Read on for growth considerations and ways to expand your reach more slowly through outsourcing.

- ❒ Read *The E-Myth*
- ❒ Decide on next actions

Notes:

To grow or not to grow?

You need to balance the freedoms you enjoy as a freelance with the limitations of hiring, premises, paperwork and keeping others happy. You don't need to grow. Be honest and touch base with your reasons for doing this work.

- ❒ Brainstorm the pros/cons of growing your business
- ❒

Notes:

Support services

Hiring a bookkeeper and accountant is typically the first step to experiencing delegation. Outsourcing jobs to someone with better skills gives you more time for your own productive work, and leads to fewer mistakes and headaches.

Next stages include graphic and web design services, virtual assistant (VA) and other remote contractors. If you have capacity, you might want to consider a trainee or intern. See the *Handbook* section on this.

- ❒ Identify tasks for potential outsourcing
- ❒ Decide next steps

Notes:

Traditional expansion

If growing your business along more traditional lines, you'll probably need an office. This will mean extra overheads, including a dedicated phone line, internet, computer, services, and insurance. So, you need to be sure extra sales will outweigh the extra cost by some distance. See the *Handbook* section on this.

- ❒ Identify pros and cons of expansion
- ❒ Decide next steps

Notes:

Partner others

Partnering with another writer allows you to take up each other's slack, pitch for bigger jobs, cover holidays, and generally support each other. Alternatively, partner with complementary creative businesses, such as graphic designers, web designers and photographers. If you find these relationships fruitful, you may want to take the next step of forming a collective.

- [ ] Brainstorm the pros and cons of growing your business

Notes:

Over to You

I hope you're now well underway with your copywriting business set-up, and are getting to grips with your workflow and processes.

Now would be a good time to reread the *Handbook,* and remind yourself of the detail. Running a business is an iterative process, so you'll need to check in with your Marketing, Operations and Writing Ninjas on a regular basis.

In the next section, you'll find Starter Projects to get you going if you don't yet have portfolio pieces. Beyond that, every freelance business is unique, so it would be great to hear from you with any questions and discoveries. I often hear from readers who have started their own successful writing businesses, and sometimes feature their questions on my blog.

In the meantime, wishing you every success with your writing business,

Jules

STARTER PROJECTS

☞ These ***Starter Projects*** are for writers who have never done paid copywriting before. They will ease you in gently, and equip you with a bunch of portfolio pieces to show clients.

This section has four assignments designed to kickstart your portfolio. Do the assignments, and you'll end up with your own leaflet and a couple of good-looking samples to show. Flushed with this success, you can then start reaching out to paid clients, and building a work pipeline.

If you're a newbie, landing your first paid client is a huge deal. You're off the blocks, and have proven that you can make money. It's a great boost to your business confidence. And it's amazing how just that one piece of evidence can open doors.

But before you get there, you need to overcome the impasse of any new business: how can you get work without a track record? And how can you get a track record without evidence of work?

The answer is to do some "calling card" or "apprentice" pieces, to build your skills and confidence, and minimize the leap to your first paid gig. The suggested steps are:

1. Do a job for yourself as client. (Off the blocks)
2. Do a real job free for someone you know. (Listening skills)
3. Do a real job free for someone you don't know. (Stranger interview skills)
4. Turn this work into portfolio samples by partnering a graphic designer. (Networking skills)

Now, it's time to dive in at the deep end with **Assignment 1**.

Assignment 1: Your Own Flyer

Your first job is to write a leaflet for yourself. The aim is to experience both sides of the process, write a job, and let it go.

With your client hat on:

You're the client, and you need a business flyer for your copywriting business. For simplicity, go for a trifold A4 or DL size – a standard format often seen in leaflet holders. Now write down your requirements:

- What's the purpose of the leaflet?
- Who's the target market?
- What's the call to action? Do you want the reader to call, email, or visit a specific page on your website?
- What tone of voice is best for your target market?
- What's your USP?
- List 3 competitor websites or promos whose look you like.
- List any relevant colours, images and logos.
- Note your contact information.
- Note how long you expect this work to take, and how much you're prepared to pay.
- Add any other questions you have for the copywriter.

With your copywriter hat on:

- Read the brief and estimate how long the job should take.
- Start your timer.
- Write the leaflet.
- Put the copy in an email to yourself, and press "send."

Some questions:

- How long did both jobs take?
- Did the client's cost expectations match the time it took you?
- How helpful was the client's brief?
- What obstacles did you encounter?

- How would you do it differently next time?
- What else did you learn?

Notes and Tips

The chances are, this took longer than you thought. You were doing this for the first time, and it's not easy to write about and for yourself.

Did you come up against perfectionist tendencies? These are helpful for editing, less so for first-drafting. To keep this in check, write to the specific wordage needed for each job. Make a physical mockup to keep the focus tight, and collect good examples to compare yours with.

Keep a note of your process. Over time, you'll be able to hone this into a system for working more effectively.

Now move on to **Assignment 2**.

Assignment 2: Flyer For a Real Client

This is a free "calling card" project. The aim is to interview someone you know, in order to practise listening and responding to client needs.

- Find a friend with a small business who needs a new flyer. Let them know that this is a freebie.
- Use your notes from **Assignment 1**, create a briefing sheet for the client.
- Ask them to fill this in and email it to you.
- Follow this up with a 10' chat to clarify any missing information.
- Estimate how long the job will take.
- Write the leaflet. Note how long it really takes.
- Email the job to the client.

Optional: Call the client for feedback. Ask for their time estimate for this kind of job.

Once again, keep notes on what you've learned for future.

Notes and Tips

Clients may not be clear about they want, even when you give them a briefing sheet. Your questions may prompt them to think about surprisingly basic matters they haven't yet articulated, including even target market and competitors.

You and clients may have an unrealistic view of the time needed. You may both enjoy talking at length about the business, but need to keep a firm handle on research time.

Optional: if you know a graphic designer or design student who owes you a favour, get your words designed, to give the client a working leaflet, and you a portfolio piece. Or, go to www.moo.com and insert your copy into one of the templates. Moo allows you to send yourself and the client a free proof without paying. If the client likes the results, they may want to go ahead to print.

Now move on to **Assignment 3a** or **3b**:

Assignment 3a: Speculative Sample

This is an unpaid, uncommissioned job for a real or imaginary client. In the creative industries, this is a common way to showcase your skills. If you know a designer in the same early-career boat as you, pair up. It could lead to a fruitful working relationship!

This time, write a larger, four-page leaflet in your preferred format. If you're working with a designer, be cautious about high-concept or unusual ideas. Small companies with small budgets often prefer not to risk out-there ideas. Companies with bigger marketing budgets may be more receptive.

To help with this assignment, use your notes from Assignment 1. You can also download a PDF on client interviews from my website (www.method-writing.com/downloads).

If you're in a hurry, cut to the chase, and do a real job for a real client.

Assignment 3b: Real Job, Real Client

A real freebie job for a real client hits several buttons at once. You'll practise the key skills of listening to the client, interpreting their brief, producing a couple of drafts, and responding to feedback. You'll hopefully also produce a piece of work which makes them happy, and does a good job of promoting their business.

Be honest with the client about your aims, and make clear this is an introductory freebie, or offer a special rate. This gives the client good value, and you a portfolio piece. Afterwards, if the client is happy, you can consider asking for a testimonial.

Assignment 4: Long Form Project

For this, write a Case Study. This is a "soft sell", informative piece that showcases an example of client work. Case studies have a substantial amount of copy, and provide a meatier example of your writing skills. They're particularly useful for business-to-business (B2B) and service companies. If you're a journalist, a case study will draw on skills you already know well: interviewing, reporting, and presenting complex topics in an accessible way.

If you like, use the same client you worked with for Assignment 3b.

Download the Case Study Template from www.method-writing.com/downloads.

Assignment 5: SEO Web Page

This project will give you a sense of the main concepts in search engine optimization (SEO). SEO can be highly technical, but understanding a few basics, such as keywords and meta descriptions, will greatly help your client work. SEO is constantly evolving in response to changing search engine algorithms, and some copywriters choose to specialize in it.

For this project, read the section on **SEO Copy**, and download the **SEO Web Page Template** from www.method-writing.com/downloads.

Assignment 6: Find a Design Collaborator

As soon as possible, get to know a professional graphic designer for ongoing collaboration – ideally a versatile one whose work you love. Graphic designers are a good source of work for freelance copywriters, and eventually, you should be able to return the favour. Find a skilled designer you get on well with, and you may have the makings of an excellent business team. Your words will look wonderful laid out in their beautiful, stylish designs, and their designs will stand out, thanks to your great copy.

If you can't find a likely graphic design professional near you, try a further education college that trains graphic design students. Students are often looking for real projects to work on, and your project may also benefit from their tutor's advice. This can be a chance to get your portfolio samples designed, and sow the seeds for future business collaboration.

Further Reading

Michael Gerber (2009)*The E-Myth*

Roger Horberry (2009) *Brilliant Copywriting*

Andy Maslen (2009) *Write To Sell: The Ultimate Guide To Great Copywriting*

Andy Maslen (2010) *The Copywriting Sourcebook: How To Write Better Copy, Faster*

Andy Maslen (2010) *Write Copy, Make Money*

Andy Maslen (2015) *Persuasive Copywriting: Using Psychology to Engage, Influence and Sell*

About Jules Horne

I'm an award-winning writer and university teacher from Scotland, where I live with my partner on the edge of the Cheviot Hills. As well as running my copywriting business, Texthouse, I teach on the MA in Creative Writing with the Open University, where I helped to write the Script strand. Like most copywriters, I've been passionate about words all my life, which led me into BBC journalism and German government translation, via a German and French degree from Oxford University. I wrote this book for the many creative writers and writing students who want to make a living from their skills.

If you've found this book helpful, visit www.method-writing.com and **sign up for my mailing list** to receive tips and templates for your copywriting business. And I'd love it if you could review this book with a short comment on Amazon – it really helps! To get in touch with me directly, email info@method-writing.com.

method writing

www.method-writing.com

Method Writing Books

www.method-writing.com

Method Writing Book 2:

Dramatic Techniques for Creative Writers

ISBN: 978-0-9934354-9-2 (paperback)

ISBN: 978-0-9934354-7-8 (ebook)

Available as audiobook on Audible.com.

Does your fiction or poetry need more oomph? Give it a boost with dramatic techniques! Discover powerful strategies from stage and screen to bring your writing fully to life.

Dramatic techniques are core narrative skills that are all about bold, clear, high-impact writing. Once you discover the industry concepts used by screen and stage writers to create stories, you'll never look back.

This practical guide to dramatic concepts will give you confidence in structure, plotting, character and editing, covering professional secrets such as:

- *dramatic action and how to use it to drive a scene*
- *how to write subtext to create tension*
- *how to use status shifts to create more dynamic characters*
- *how to use objects to focus character relationships*
- *how to use space for impact and tension*
- *how transformations can make your storytelling more dynamic*
- *the difference between private and public settings in story dynamics*
- *how the ribbon of time can help tight, powerful editing*
- *how to use rituals to shortcut exposition*

Discover dramatic techniques and take your writing to another level!

Method Writing Book 3:

Writing for Audiobooks

ISBN: 978-1-9164960-1-9 (paperback)
ISBN: 978-1-9164960-0-2 (ebook)
Available as audiobook on Audible.com.

Are you an author interested in audiobooks? Want to get your fiction or non-fiction book ready for the fastest-growing publishing market? Voice-first writing skills are a must if you want to make your book really shine on the audio platform.

Whether you're an author, publisher, narrator, or preparing your own book for voiceover narration, *Writing for Audiobooks* will get you audio-ready! Pack with radio writing advice for fiction, non-fiction and scripts.

> *"Audiobooks are the fastest-growing segment in publishing, but writing for audio first is a skill that few writers have needed to learn. Until now. If you want to make sure your writing resonates for this growing audience, Jules's book will give you useful tips for adjusting your words and reaching listeners. Highly recommended!"*
>
> Joanna Penn, The Creative Penn

Excerpt from *Writing for Audiobooks*

Audiobooks are enjoying an exciting boom, and it's set to continue and grow.

More and more people are listening to audiobooks in preference to reading. Major publishers are reporting 20-30% increases in audiobook sales. And some are commissioning straight-to-audio fiction.

So if you're a writer, this is a big deal. The book market is shifting towards audio, and you need to be part of it.

However, not every book is great for audio. Not every writer knows about audio writing techniques. Those that do will find their books make an easy transition. The writing will be more fun for narrators to read, and clearer and more compelling for listeners to hear.

Writing for the ear calls for specific skills. Skills that are well known in the worlds of radio, performance, and spoken word. But far less familiar in the world of traditional books.

Since audiobooks are on the rise, it makes sense for writers to learn those skills, and soon.

I'm particularly excited because I'm a fiction writer with a professional background in radio. I've written for stage, and performed spoken word in English and Scots. The rhythms and music of spoken word are in my writing DNA anyway.

And suddenly, the extra techniques I've learned from radio and stage writing have turned out to be very useful indeed.

They're easy to learn, and they'll transform your impact as an audiobook author.

You may even decide to join the many authors now writing with audio-first in mind.

This is a handbook for anyone interested in audio writing – writing for the ear, writing for performance.

If you're traditionally published, you'll learn audio writing strategies and be well prepared for this growing and lucrative market.

If you're an indie author, you'll learn how to prepare your books for audio recording and what to consider when working with a narrator or narrating your own book.

I'll be covering, among other things:

- How do you write for the audio platform?
- What's different about writing for the ear, rather than the eye?
- How do you deal with visual elements such as URLs, images, graphs, tables, headers?
- Can audio-first writing improve your book for listeners?

The answer is "yes". Of course!

The written and spoken word are very different media, as you'll discover. And audio is tremendous fun!

So, who's this book for?

Anyone who wants to up their writing game, and polish their books for better audio impact.

Fiction authors – both traditionally published and indie – who are interested in this booming market for storytellers.

Non-fiction authors wondering how to adapt their books for audio.

Teachers of professional writing who want an overview of audio-specific writing skills.

Early adopters excited by audiobooks. Hopefully, that's you!

But first, a story.

I was a young, newly published fiction writer. I'd even won a prize and was feeling pretty pleased with myself. And I'd just written my first playscript, and was in my first rehearsal, waiting for my beautiful words to be beautifully read by actors.

So I was shocked by what happened next.

The actors – very experienced and one even rather famous – were running out of breath. My lines were too long. Full of qualifying clauses. Piled-on adjectives. Some bits weren't even quite logical.

Now, I'd worked very hard on that script. It was well written, and well edited. But as a script for performance, it didn't work.

Wow - did I sharpen up after that! Every word had to be weighed and counted.

An audiobook is a script. Your narrator makes it a performance. And that alone calls for different writing skills.

So, some of what follows comes from the world of performance. Some of it comes from my BBC training in radio news. Some of it comes from teaching many aspiring and inspiring writers as a tutor for the Open University.

Most of the techniques are straightforward, and you can put them into practice right away. I've gathered some of the main ones in a download on my website – see the link at the end of this book.

Others go deeper into what's different about ears, linear thinking and audio flow – including hooks and arcs that keep things moving forward.

Rest assured: you don't need to change your writing voice – simply get some extra editing and structuring skills to help listeners who'll hear your story only once. Skills that are great, as it happens, for your editing in general.

Audio offers an amazing sense of connection. The intimacy of voices in your ear, the music, rhythm and humanity of different and distinctive ways of telling stories.

You may find that the spoken word is more natural for you, and your writing can flourish in audio form.

If you already write spoken word, performance poetry, dialect or scripts, maybe audiobooks are your natural home!

Audio is different.

Publishers, readers and writers are just beginning to discover its full potential.

It's a fascinating time, and exciting to be part of it....

Printed in Great Britain
by Amazon

65268677R00068